Vegetable Group

by Megan Borgert-Spaniol

BELLWETHER MEDIA · MINNEAPOLIS, MN

Note to Librarians, Teachers, and Parents:

Blastoff! Readers are carefully developed by literacy experts and combine standards-based content with developmentally appropriate text.

Level 1 provides the most support through repetition of high-frequency words, light text, predictable sentence patterns, and strong visual support.

Level 2 offers early readers a bit more challenge through varied simple sentences, increased text load, and less repetition of high-frequency words.

Level 3 advances early-fluent readers toward fluency through increased text and concept load, less reliance on visuals, longer sentences, and more literary language.

Level 4 builds reading stamina by providing more text per page, increased use of punctuation, greater variation in sentence patterns, and increasingly challenging vocabulary.

Level 5 encourages children to move from "learning to read" to "reading to learn" by providing even more text, varied writing styles, and less familiar topics.

Whichever book is right for your reader, Blastoff! Readers are the perfect books to build confidence and encourage a love of reading that will last a lifetime!

This edition first published in 2012 by Bellwether Media, Inc.

No part of this publication may be reproduced in whole or in part without written permission of the publisher. For information regarding permission, write to Bellwether Media, Inc., Attention: Permissions Department, 5357 Penn Avenue South, Minneapolis, MN 55419.

Library of Congress Cataloging-in-Publication Data
Borgert-Spaniol, Megan, 1989-
 Vegetable group / by Megan Borgert-Spaniol.
  p. cm. – (Blastoff! readers. Eating right with myplate)
 Summary: "Relevant images match informative text in this introduction to the vegetable group. Intended for students in kindergarten through third grade"– Provided by publisher.
 Includes bibliographical references and index.
 ISBN 978-1-60014-760-9 (hardcover : alk. paper)
 1. Vegetables in human nutrition–Juvenile literature. 2. Vegetables–Juvenile literature. I. Title.
 QP144.V44B67 2012
 613.2–dc23   2011033121

Printed in the United States of America, North Mankato, MN.

010112   1207

Contents

The Vegetable Group

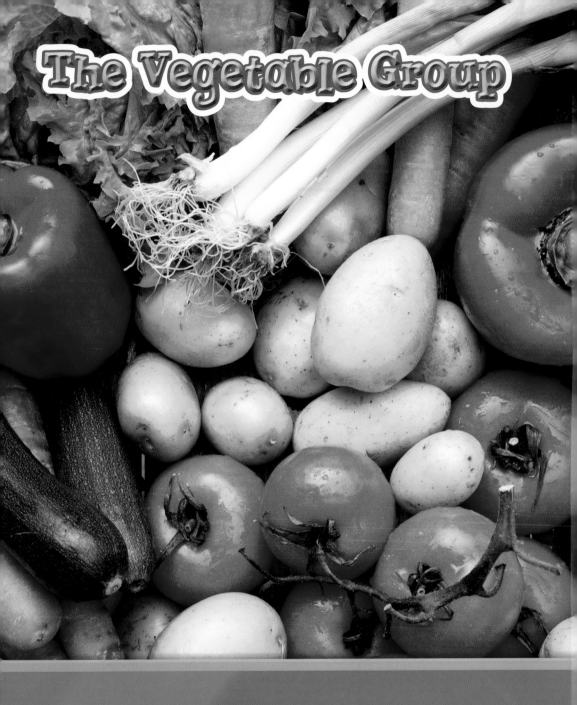

Vegetables and 100% vegetable juices belong to the Vegetable Group.

Part of Plant	Vegetables
Root...........	Carrots Potatoes Radishes
Stem...........	Asparagus Celery Rhubarb
Leaves.........	Cabbage Lettuce Spinach
Fruit...........	Eggplant Peppers Squash
Seeds..........	Beans Corn Peas
Flower.........	Artichoke Broccoli Cauliflower

Vegetables come from all the different parts of a plant.

Fruits

Grains

Dairy

Vegetables

Protein

The green part of **MyPlate** is the Vegetable Group.

1 serving = 12 baby carrots
2 large celery stalks
1 large tomato
1 baked potato
1 ear of corn
1 large pepper

Kids need one and a half servings of vegetables each day.

Why Are Vegetables Good For You?

Different vegetables have different benefits for your body.

8

Carrots and sweet potatoes are rich in **vitamin A**. This is good for your eyes and skin.

Broccoli, cauliflower, and bell peppers have **vitamin C**.

Vitamin C keeps your teeth and **gums** healthy. It also helps your body heal.

Potatoes and tomatoes are full of **potassium**. This gives you energy to play.

12

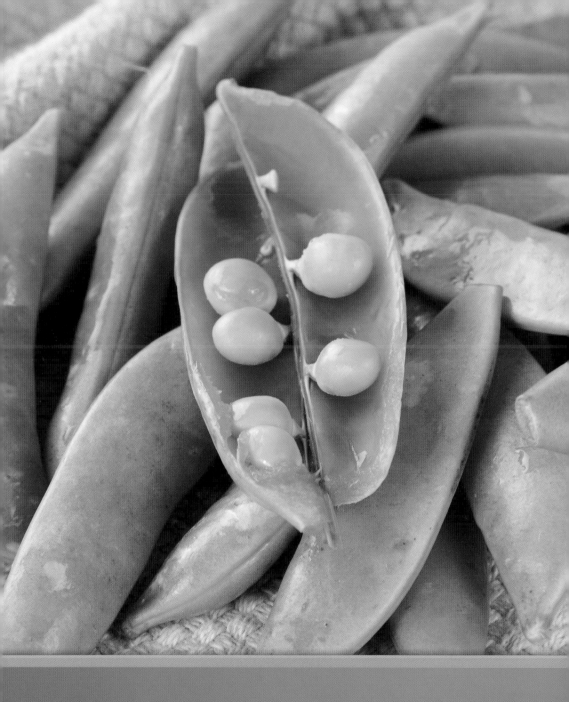

Fiber helps move food through your body. Spinach and peas are high in fiber.

Choosing Vegetables

Vegetables can be raw,
frozen, or canned.

Canned vegetables are often high in **sodium**. Choose raw vegetables when you can.

15

Eating Vegetables

Vegetables can be a tasty part of every meal. Make a vegetable **omelet** for breakfast.

Try squash soup for lunch.
Have sweet potato fries for
an afternoon snack.

17

You can make your own
spaghetti sauce with tomatoes
and other vegetables.

Strawberry rhubarb crisp and carrot cake are sweet desserts made with vegetables.

Pick a new vegetable to try every week.

Remember to fill your plate
with vegetables of every color!

Glossary

fiber—the part of a plant that stays whole as it moves through your body

gums—the soft, pink tissues that hold your teeth in place

MyPlate—a guide that shows the kinds and amounts of food you should eat each day

omelet—a dish made of eggs that are cooked until firm; omelets are usually filled with cheese and vegetables.

potassium—a part of some foods that keeps your muscles healthy and gives you energy

sodium—salt; too much sodium is bad for your heart and blood.

vitamin A—a part of some foods that is good for your eyes and skin

vitamin C—a part of some foods that helps keep your teeth and gums healthy; vitamin C also helps your body heal.

To Learn More

AT THE LIBRARY

Ehlert, Lois. *Eating the Alphabet: Fruits & Vegetables from A to Z*. San Diego, Calif.: Harcourt, 2006.

Gibbons, Gail. *The Vegetables We Eat*. New York, N.Y.: Holiday House, 2007.

Lin, Grace. *The Ugly Vegetables*. Watertown, Mass.: Charlesbridge, 1999.

ON THE WEB

Learning more about the Vegetable Group is as easy as 1, 2, 3.

1. Go to www.factsurfer.com.

2. Enter "Vegetable Group" into the search box.

3. Click the "Surf" button and you will see a list of related Web sites.

With factsurfer.com, finding more information is just a click away.

Index

The images in this book are reproduced through the courtesy of: Juan Martinez, front cover, pp. 5, 7, 10; Gilles Lougassi, p. 4; U.S. Department of Agriculture, Center for Nutrition Policy and Promotion, p. 6; Sarsmis, p. 8; Monkey Business Images, pp. 9, 15; Paul Bradbury / Getty Images, p. 11; Kzenon, p. 12; Mark Stout Photography, p. 13; Jiri Hera, p. 14; Anna Hoychuk, p. 16; Nancy Kennedy, p. 17; Gelpi, p. 18; RoJo Images, p. 19; Imagesource / Photolibrary, pp. 20-21.